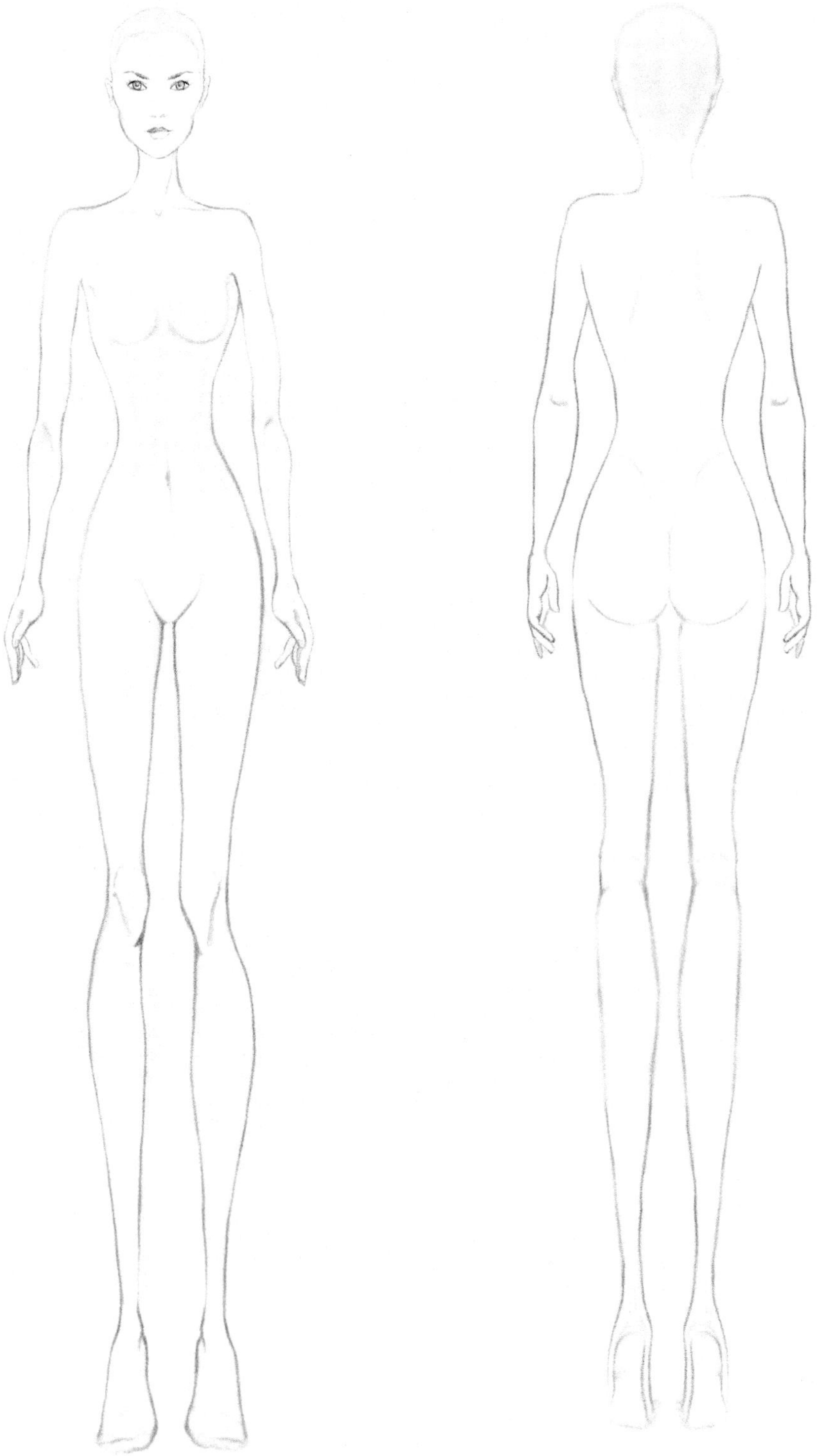

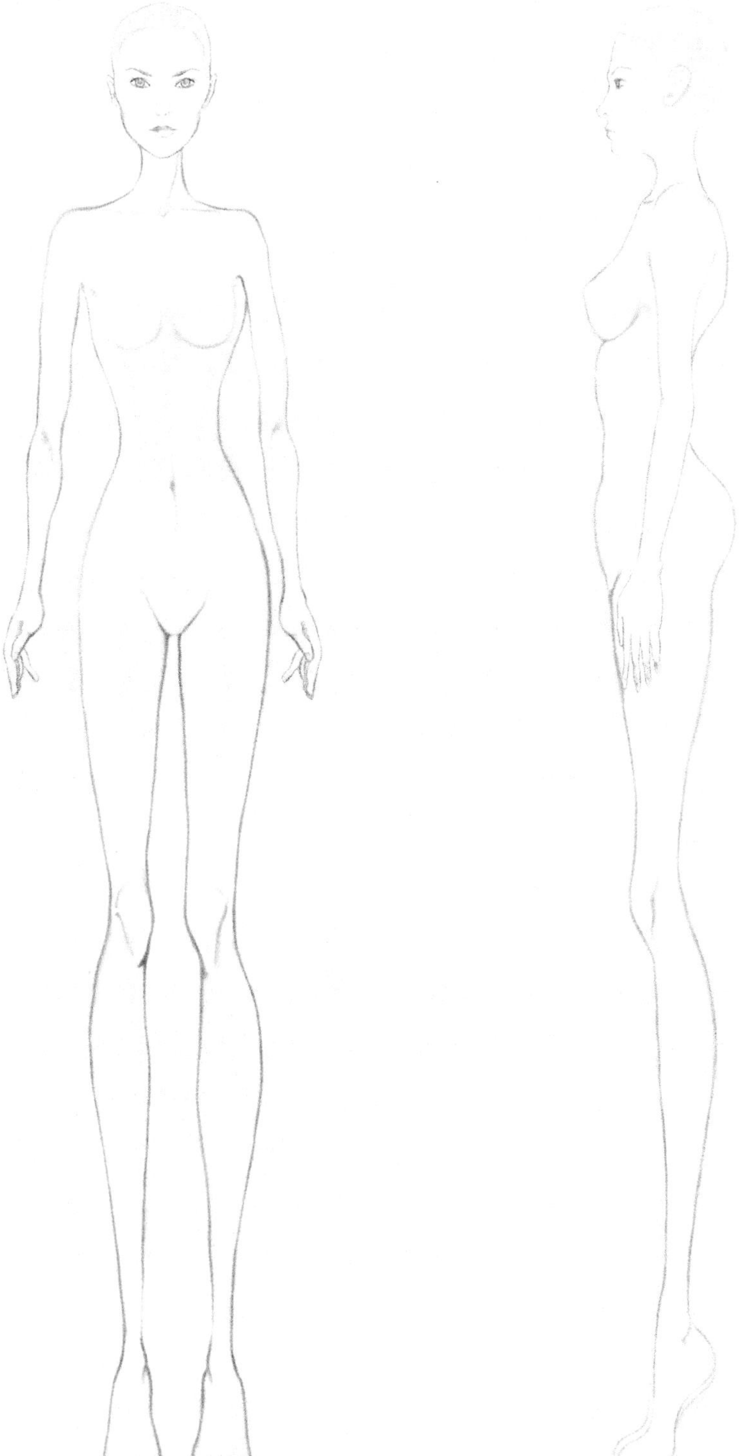

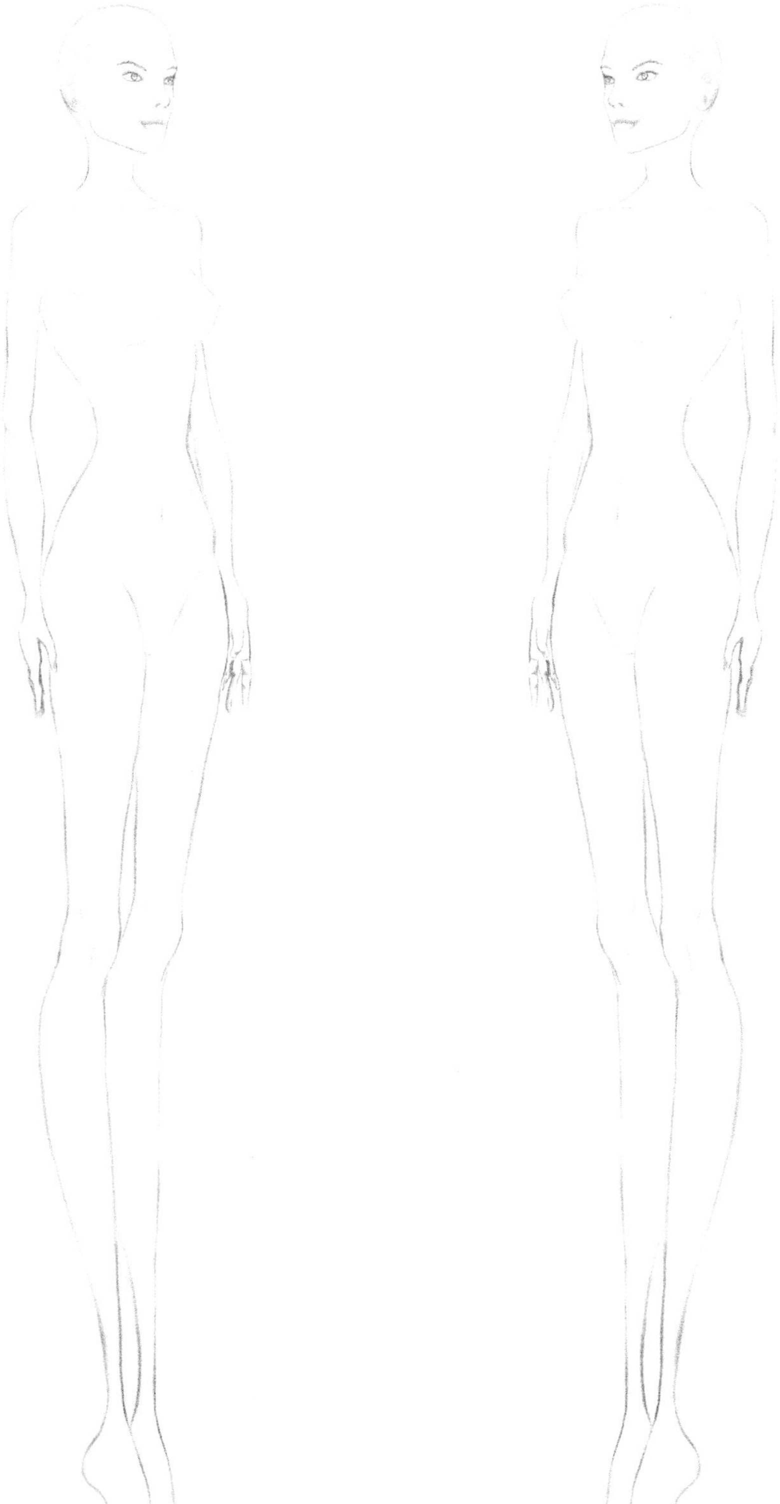

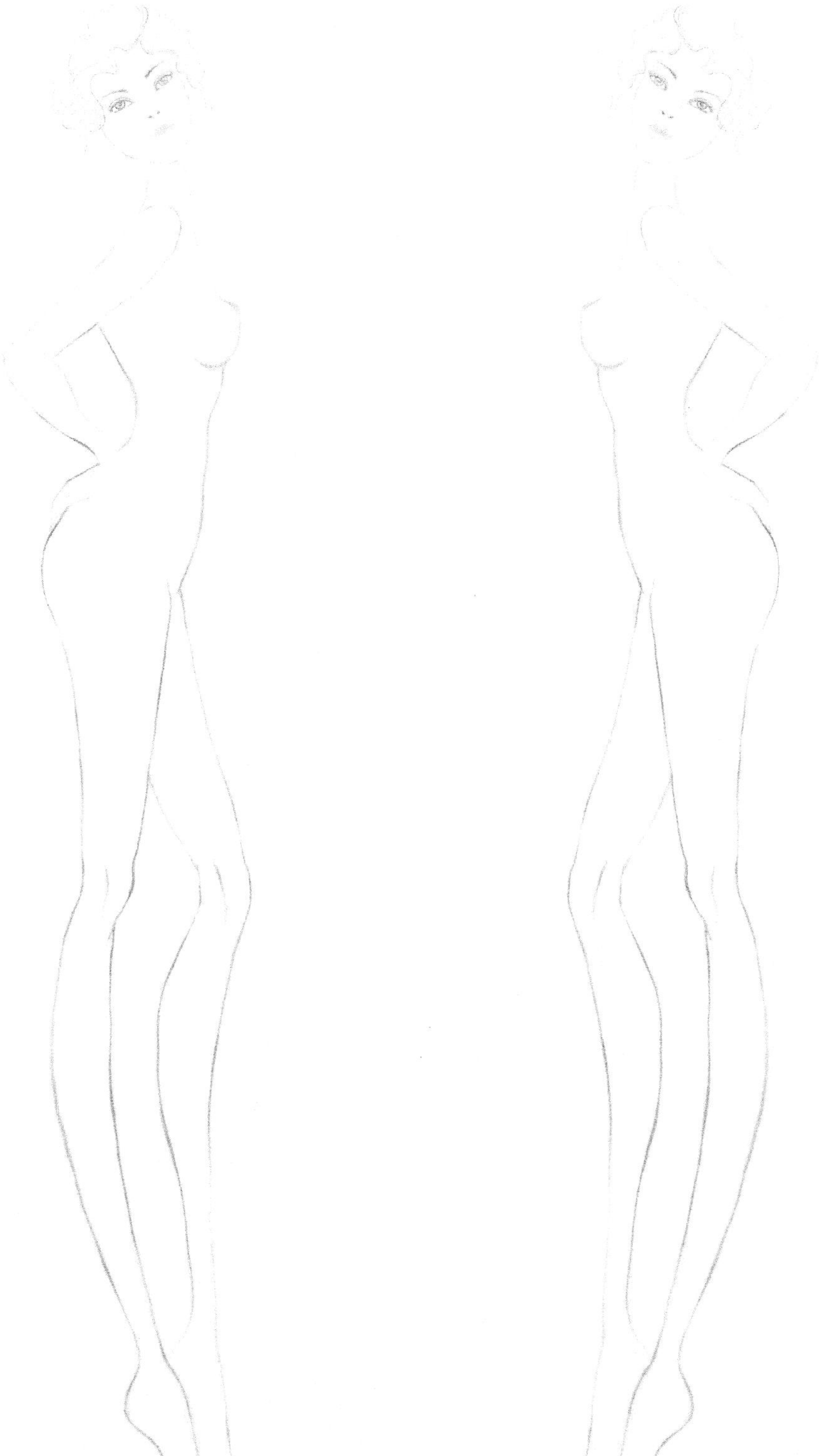

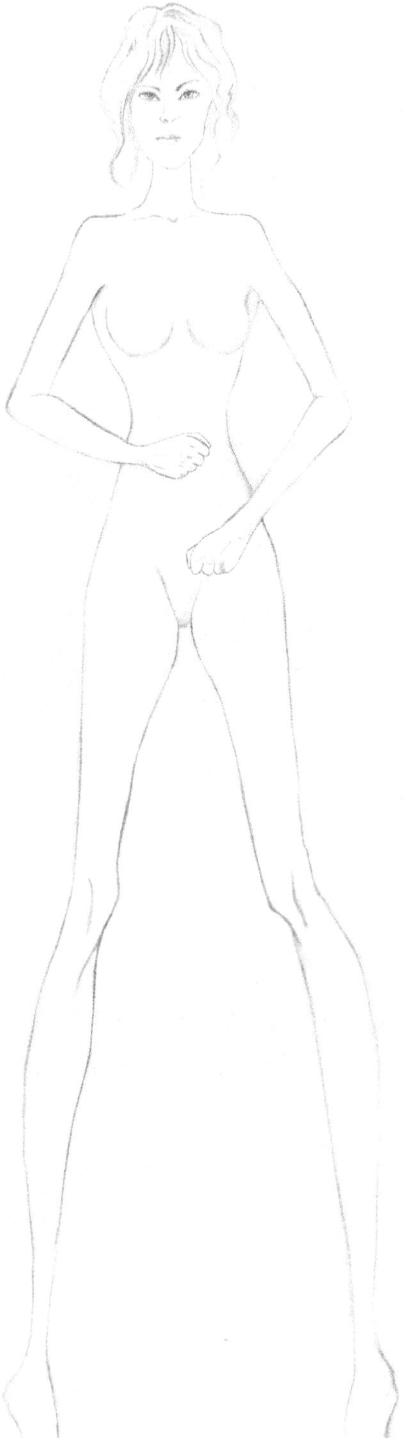

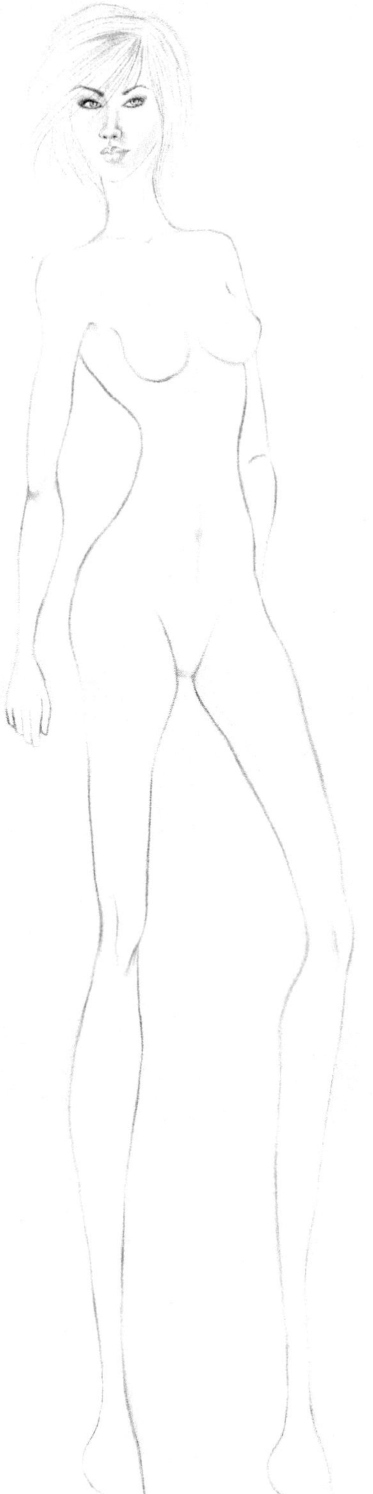

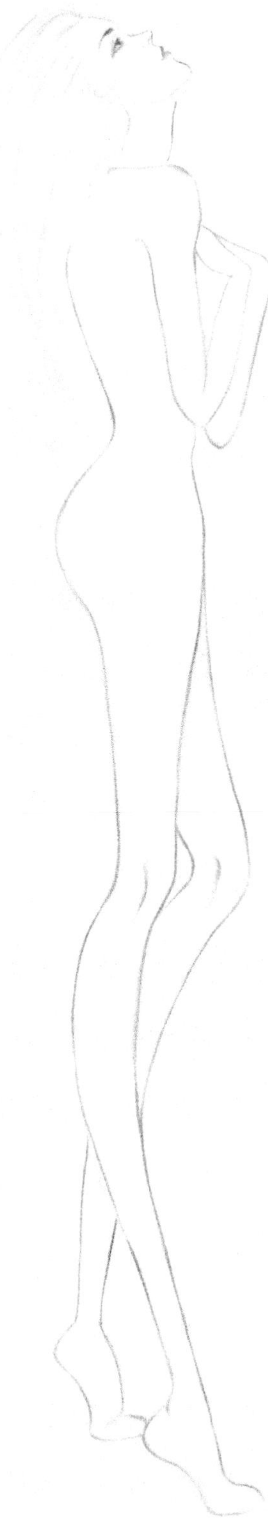

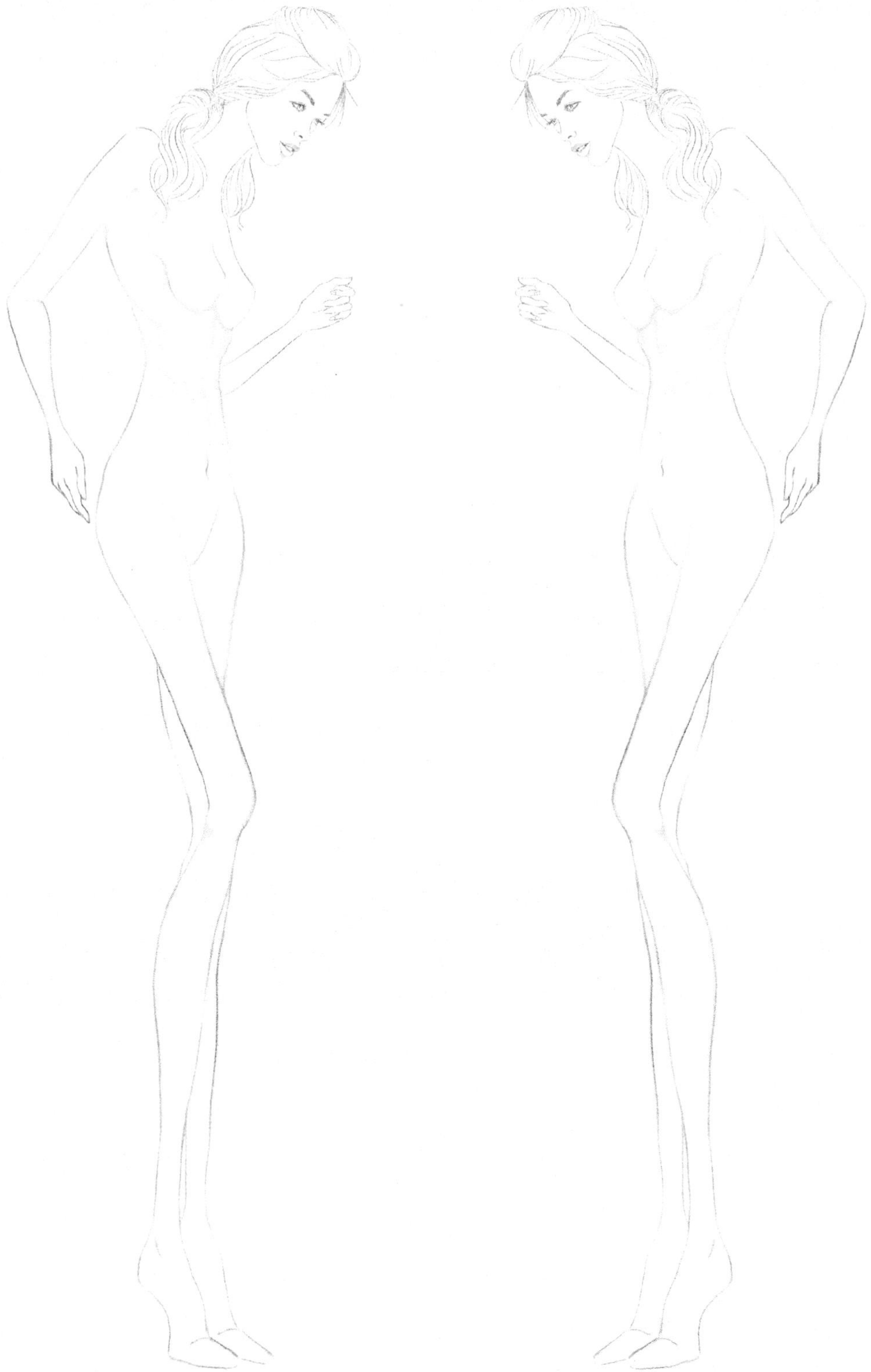

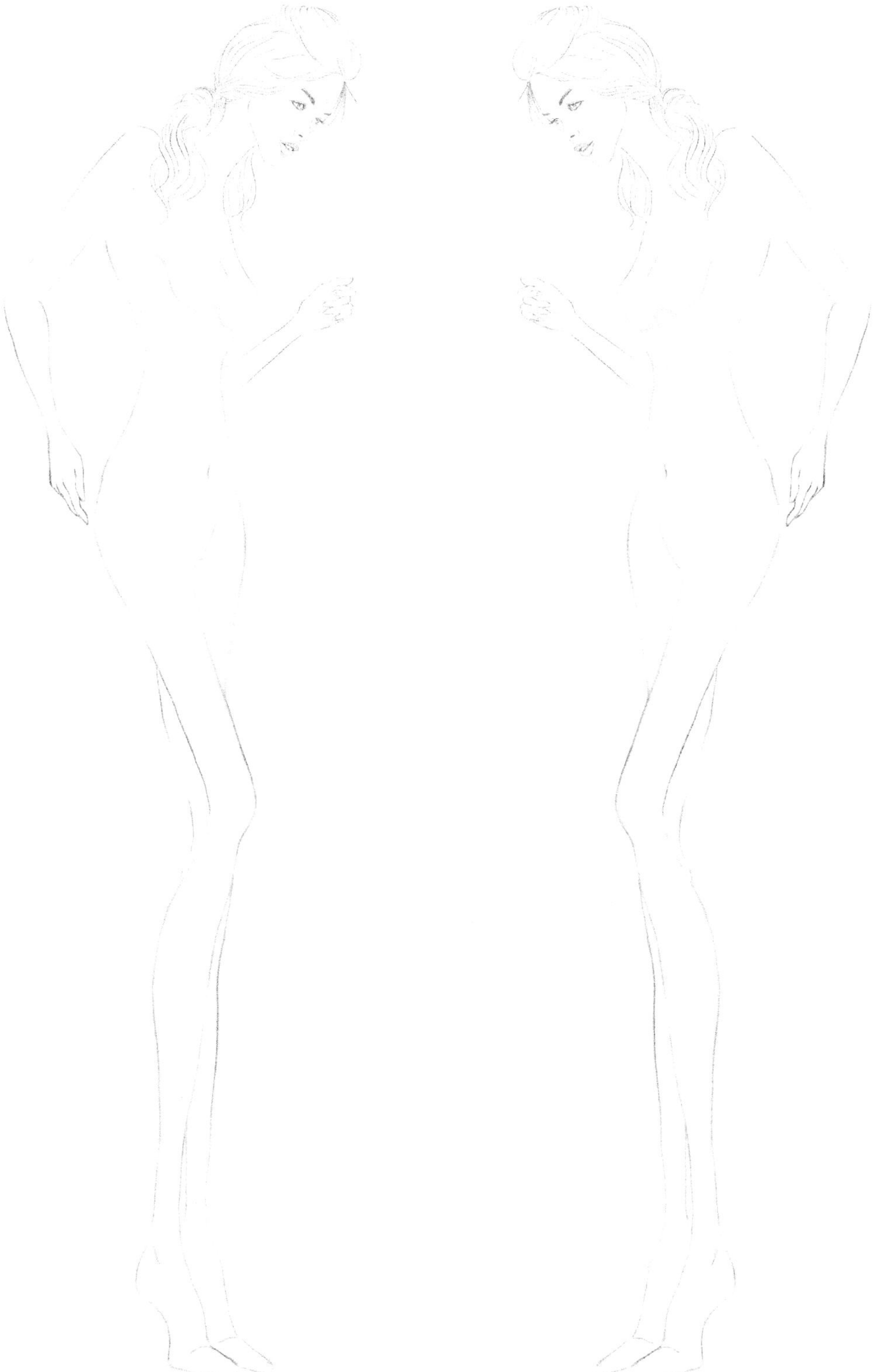

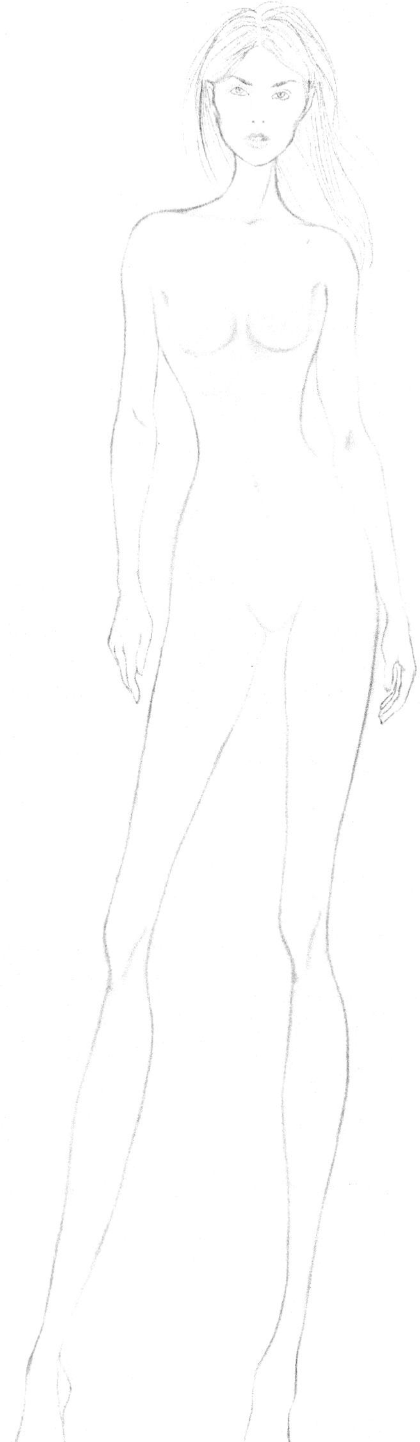

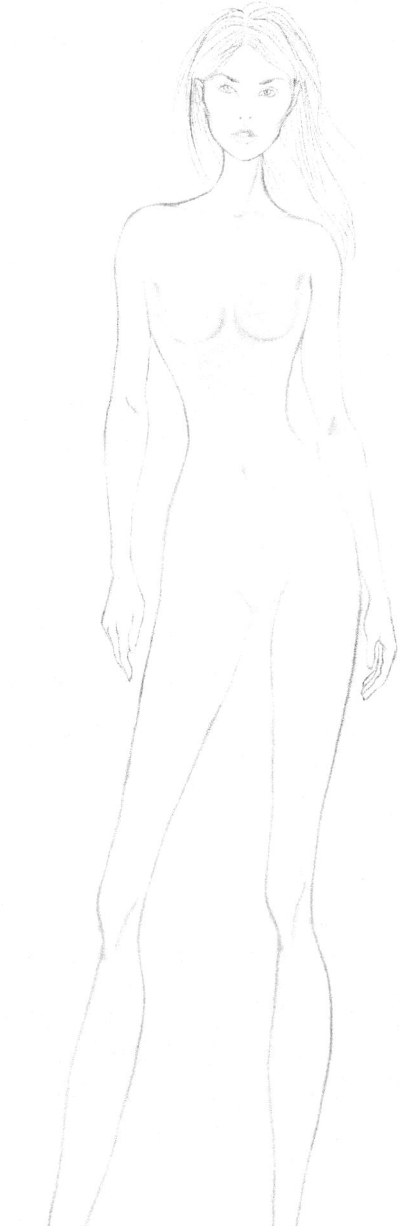

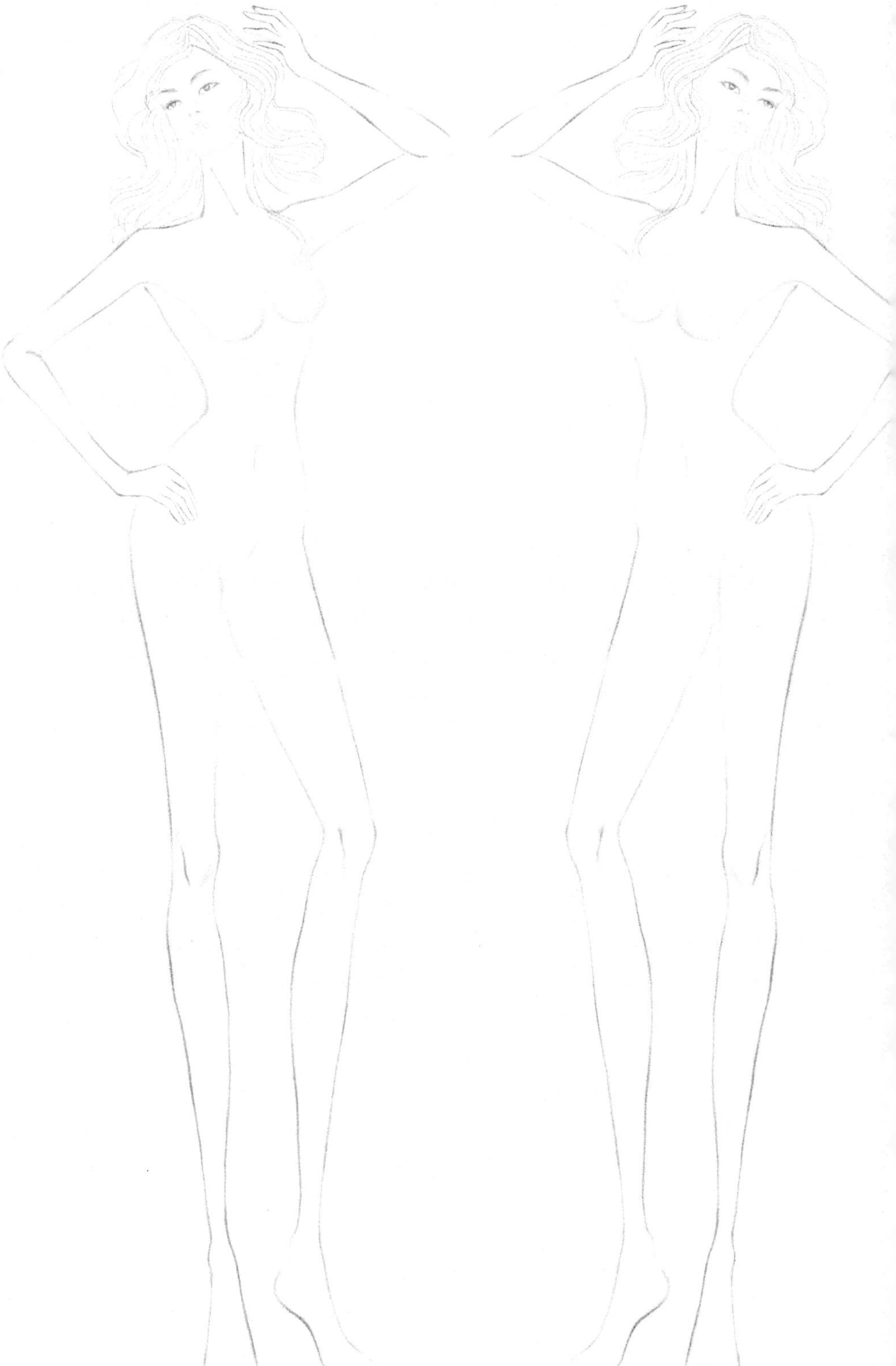

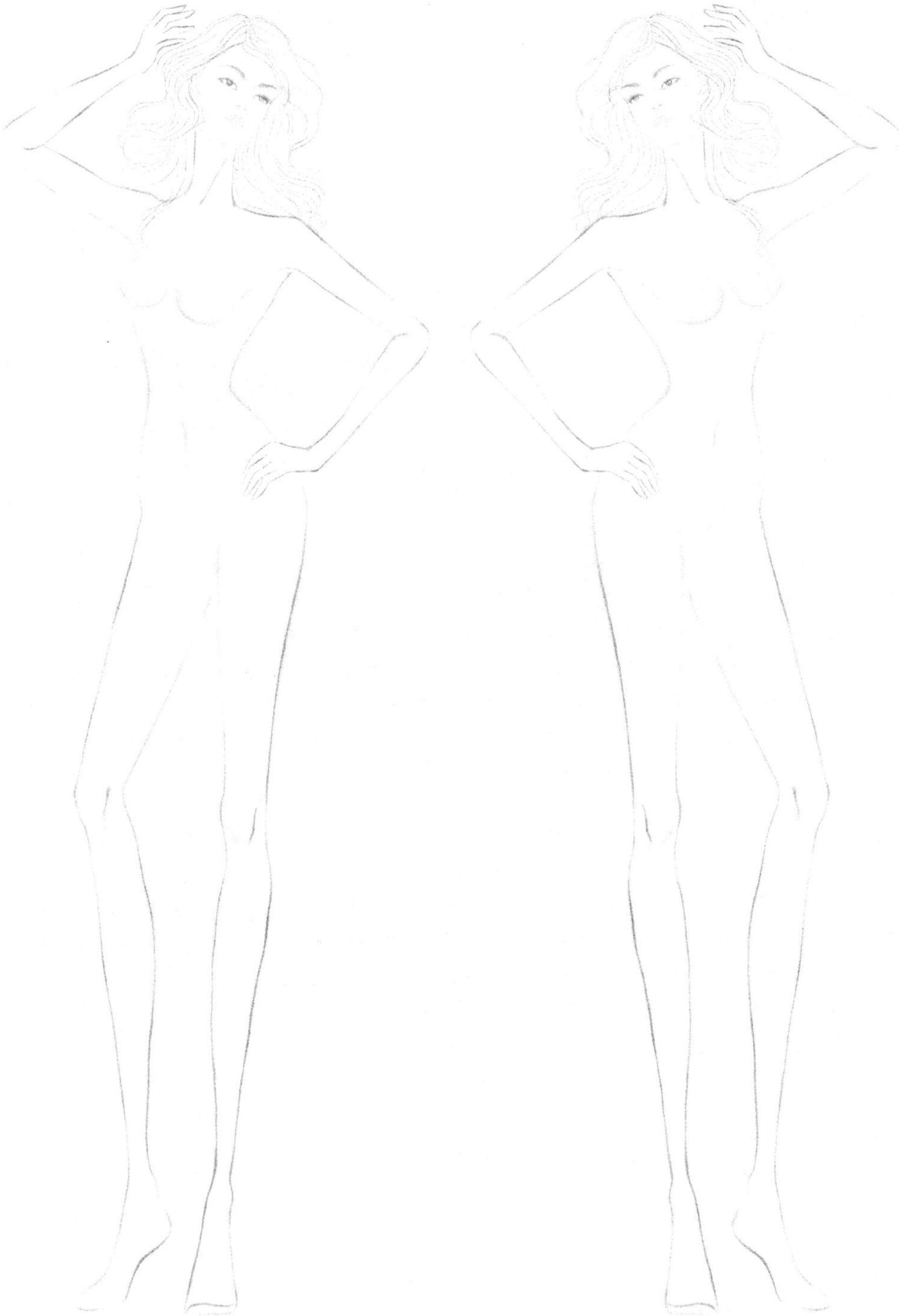

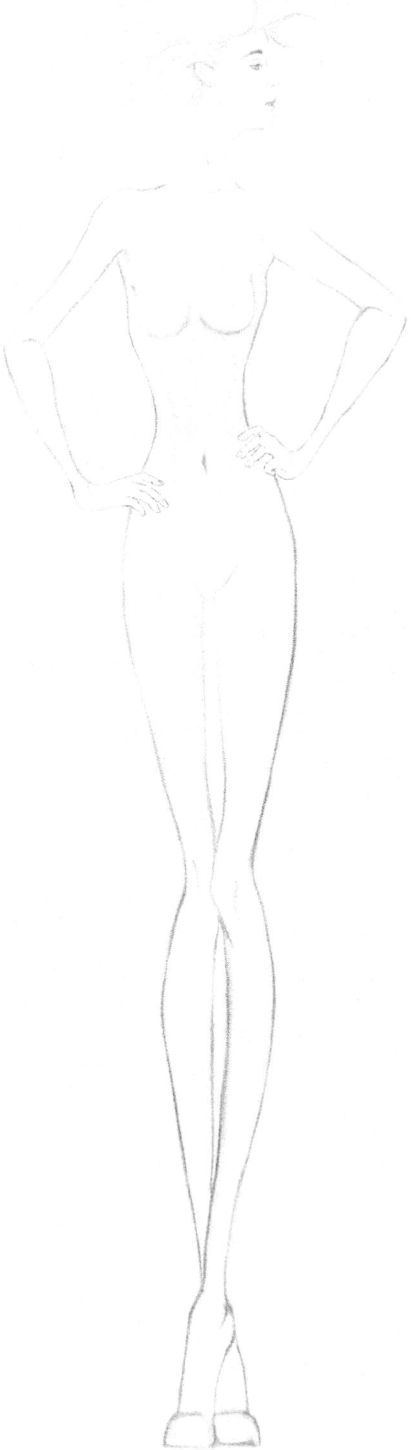

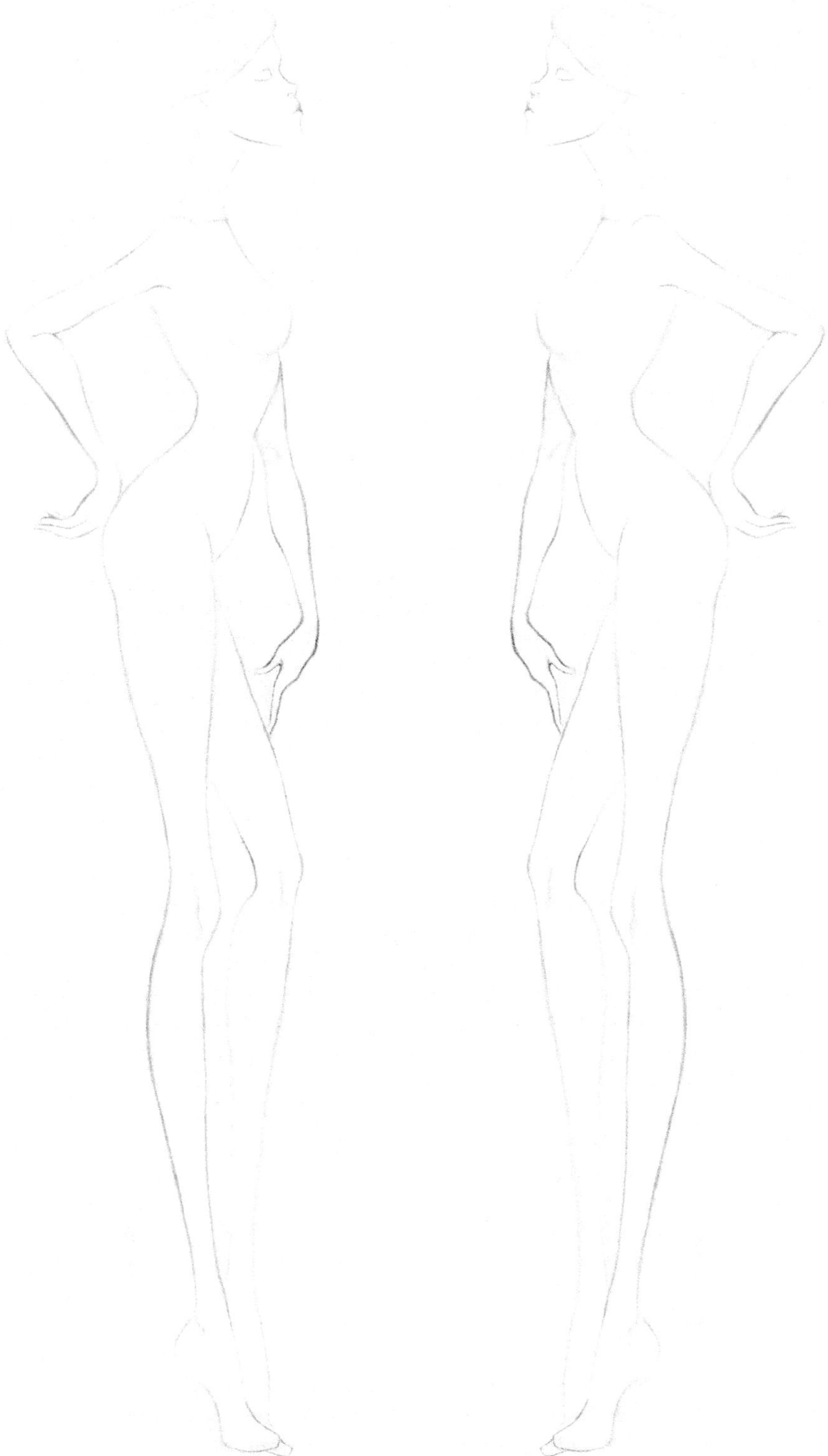

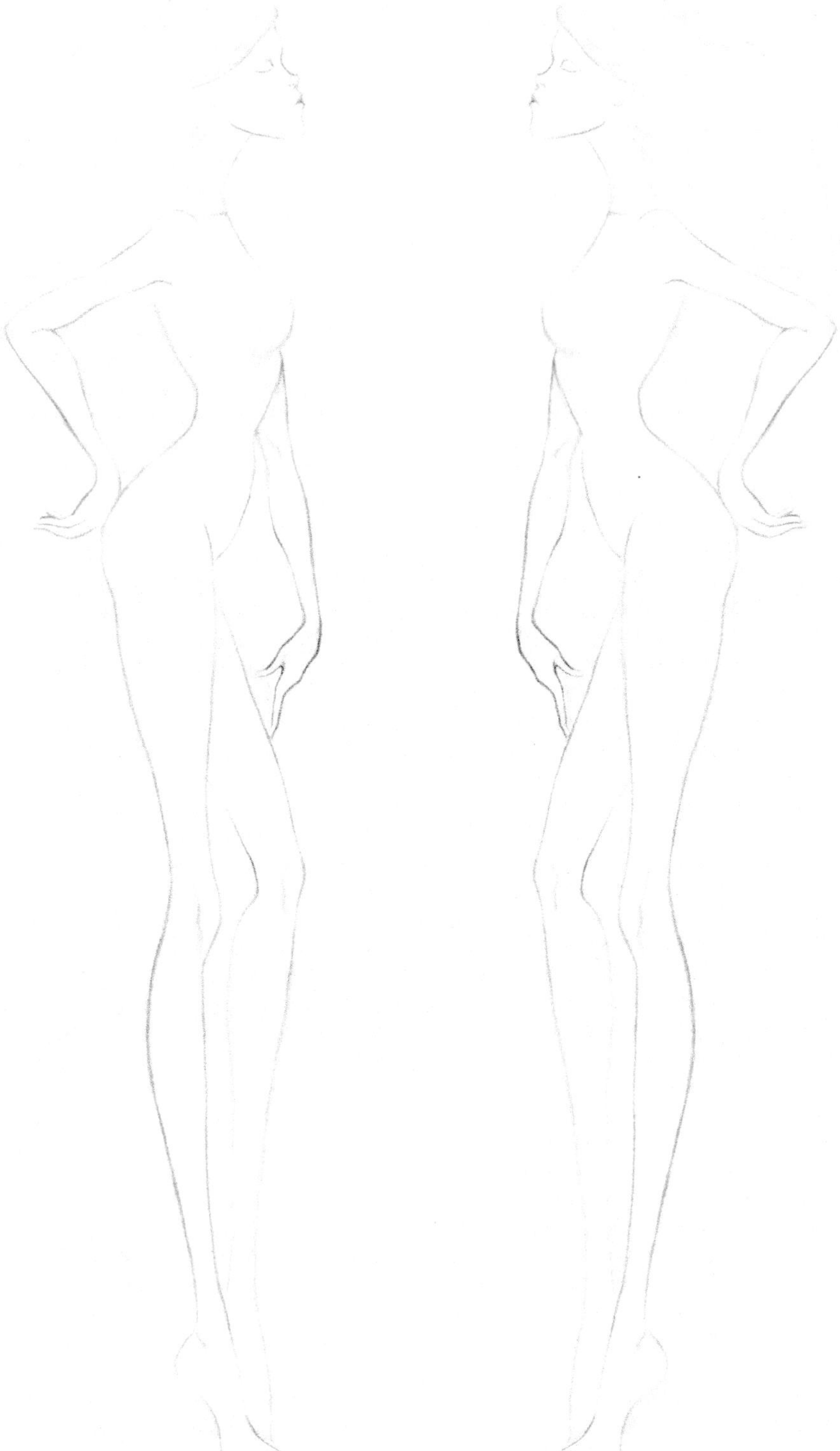

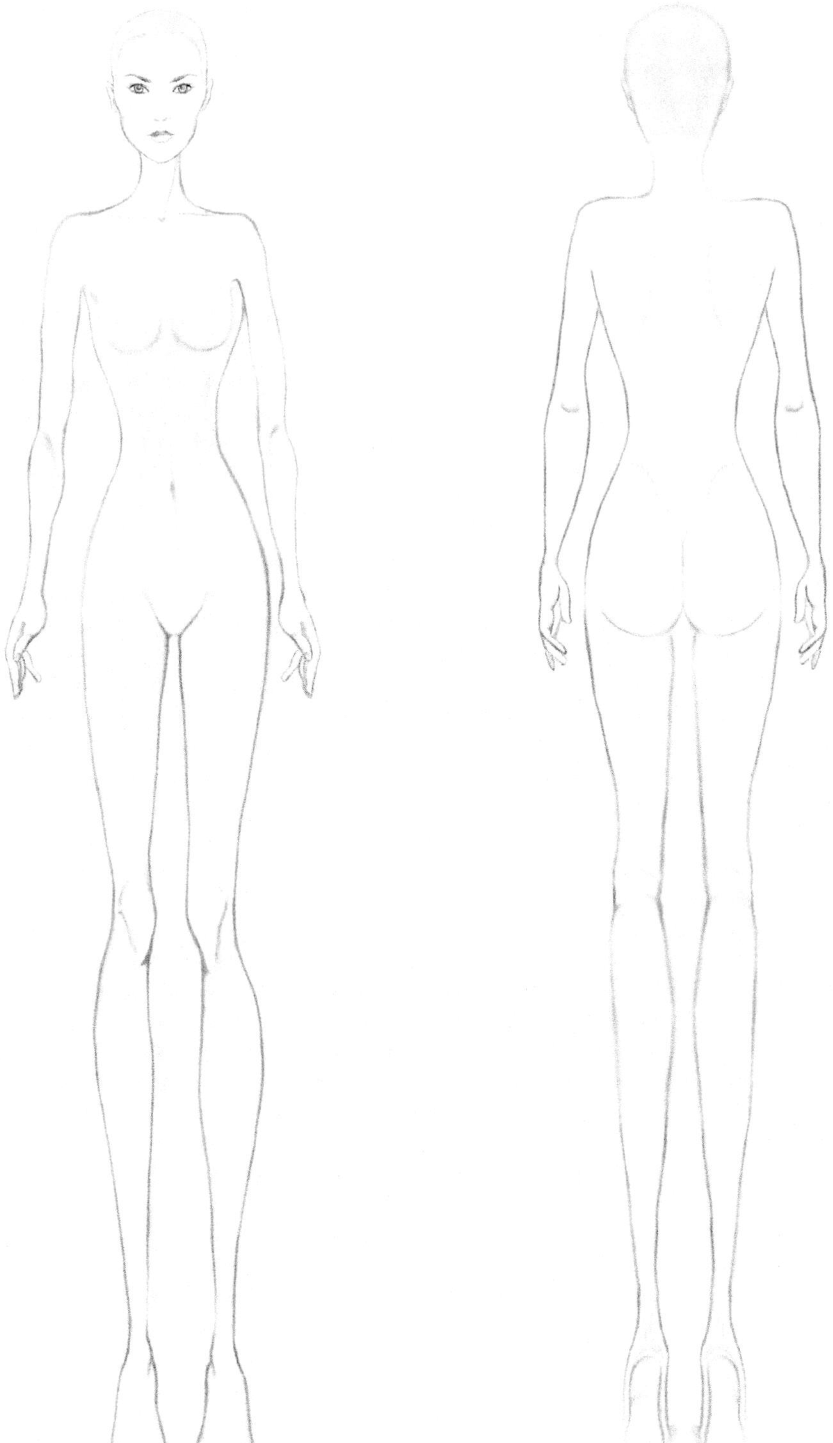

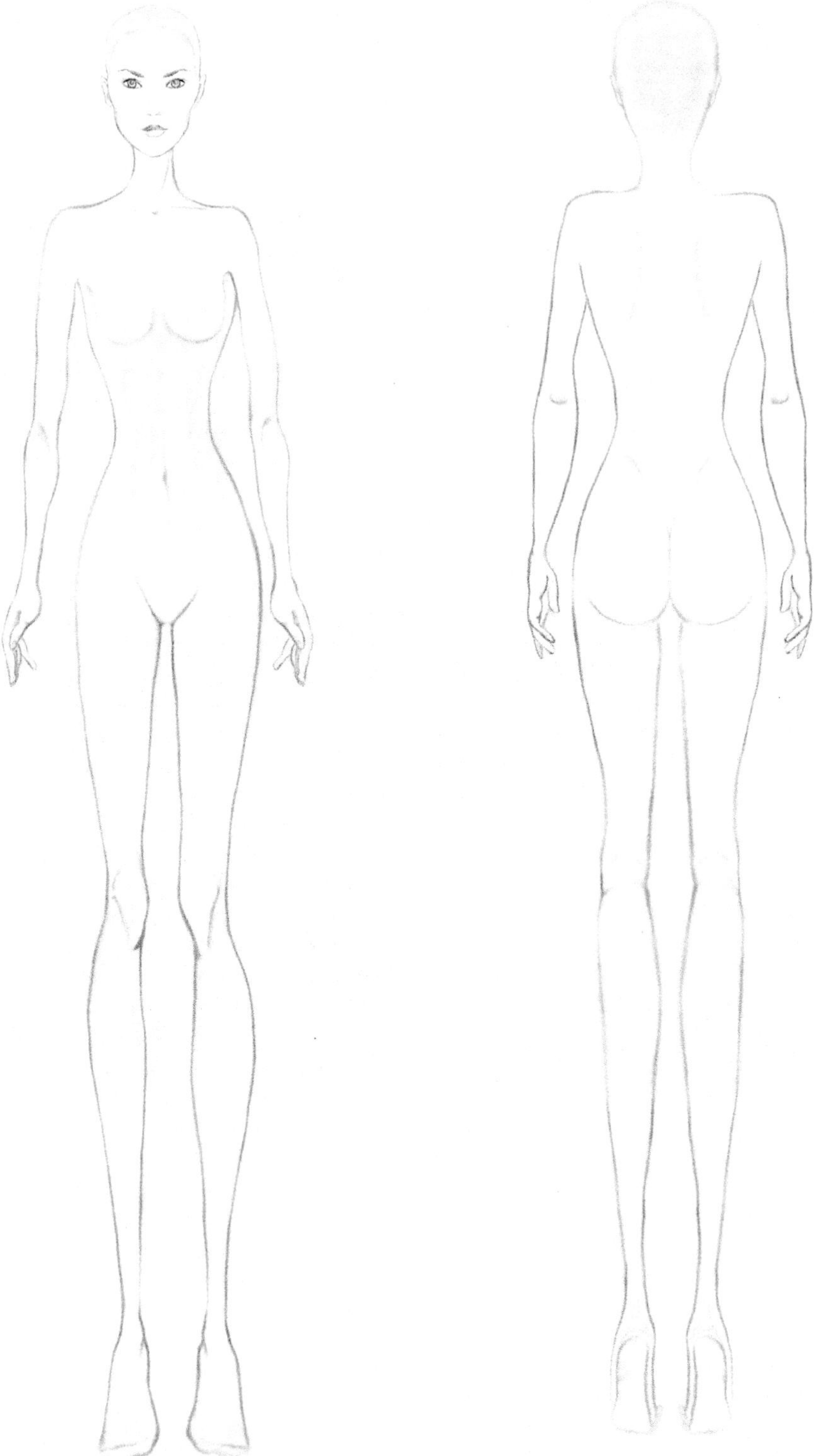

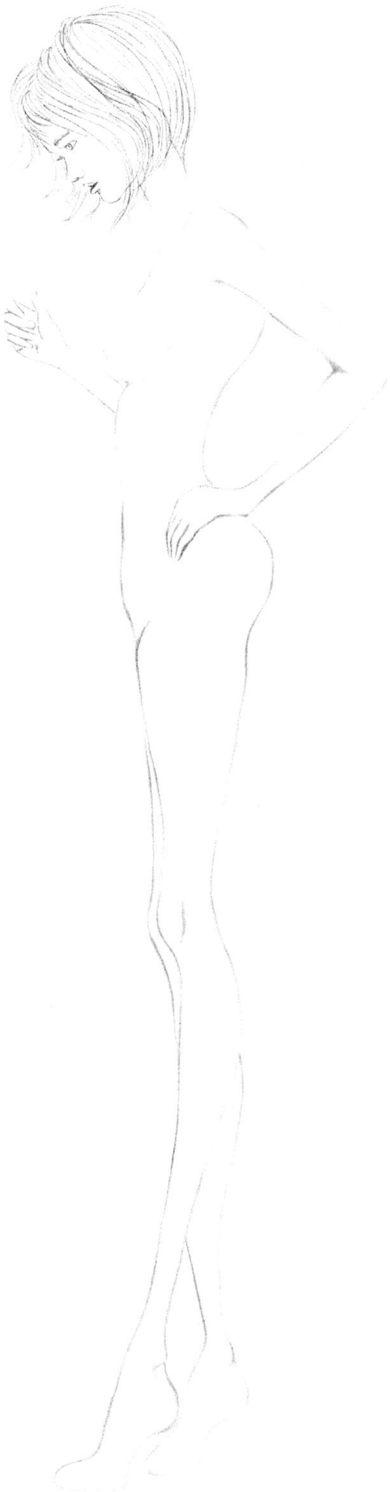

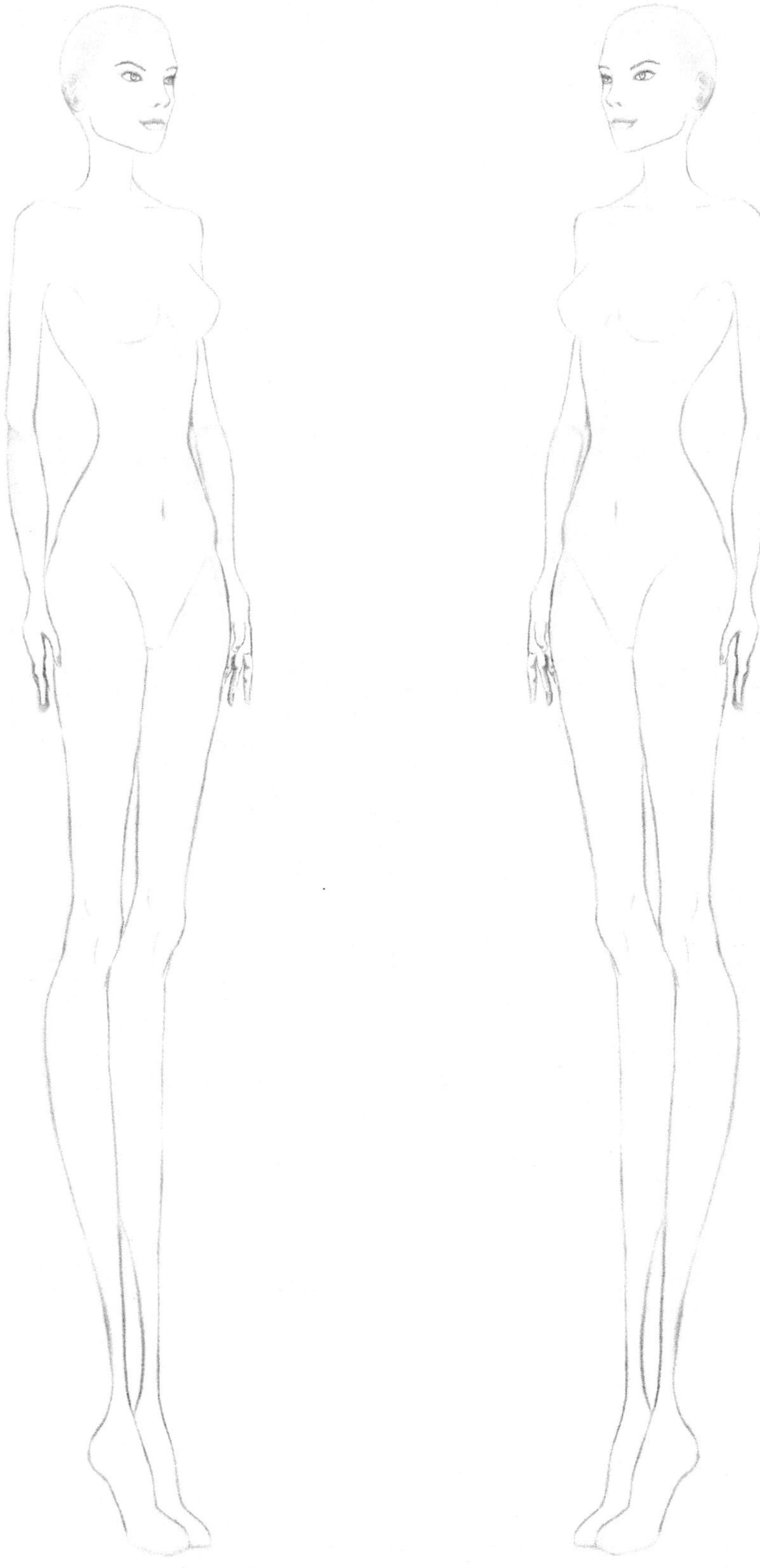

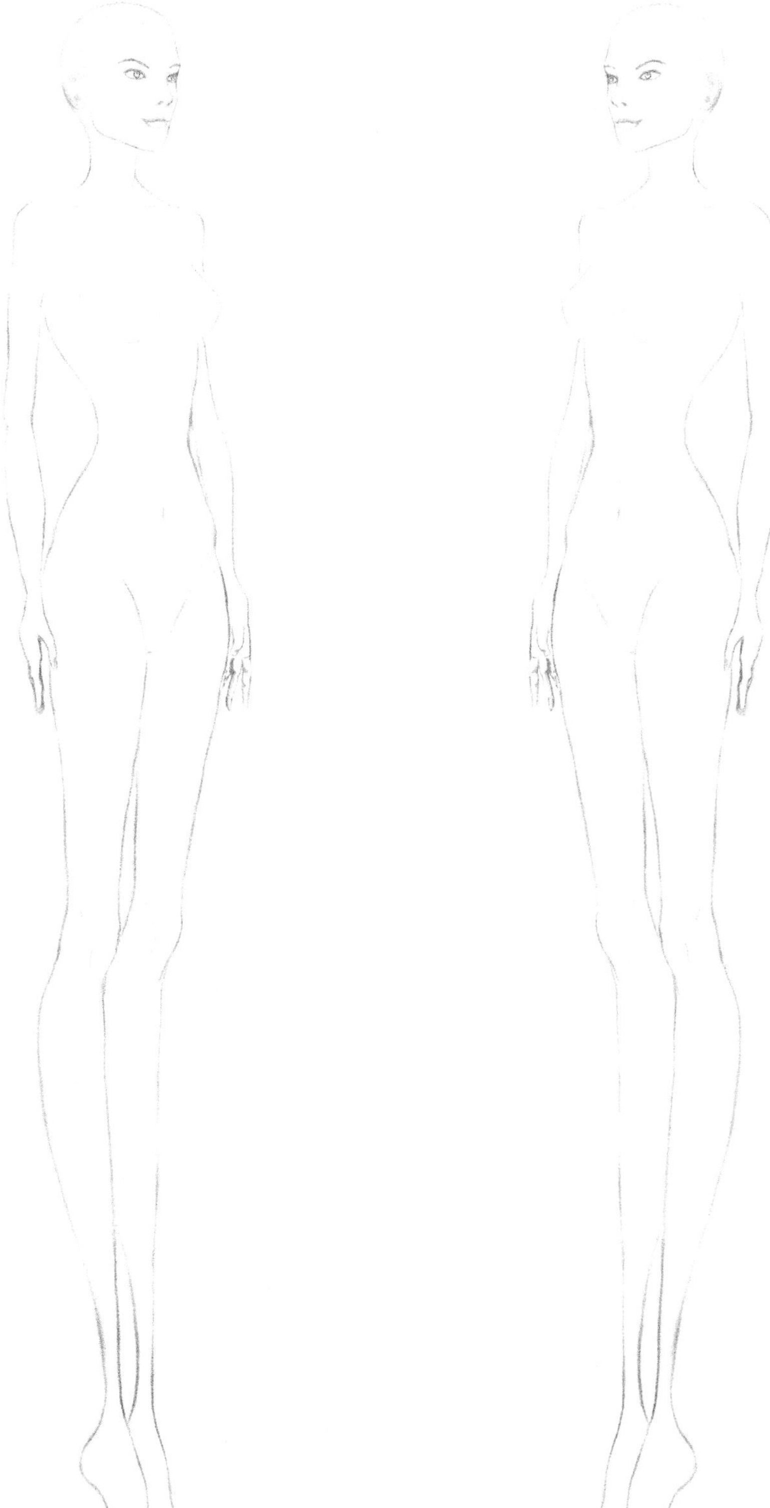

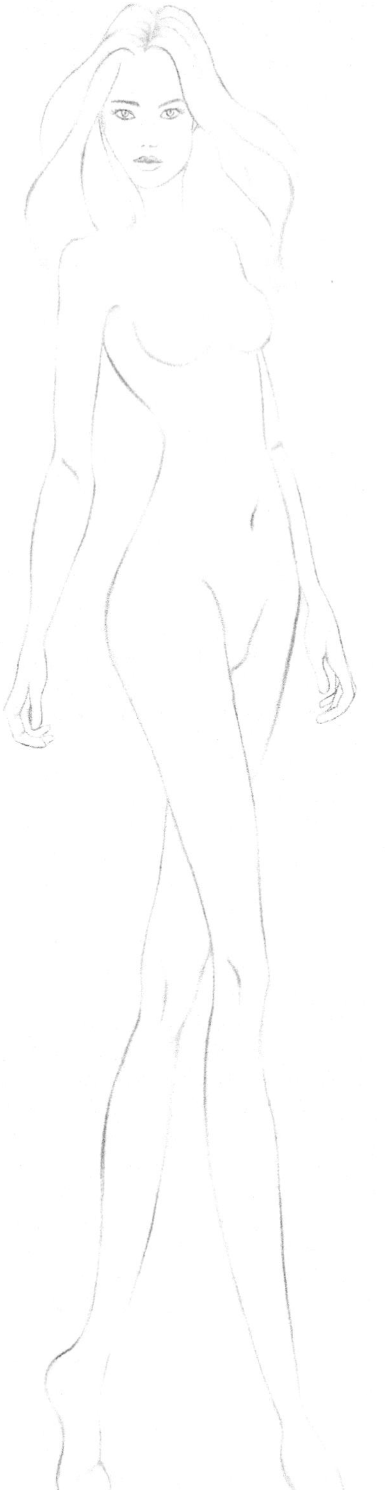

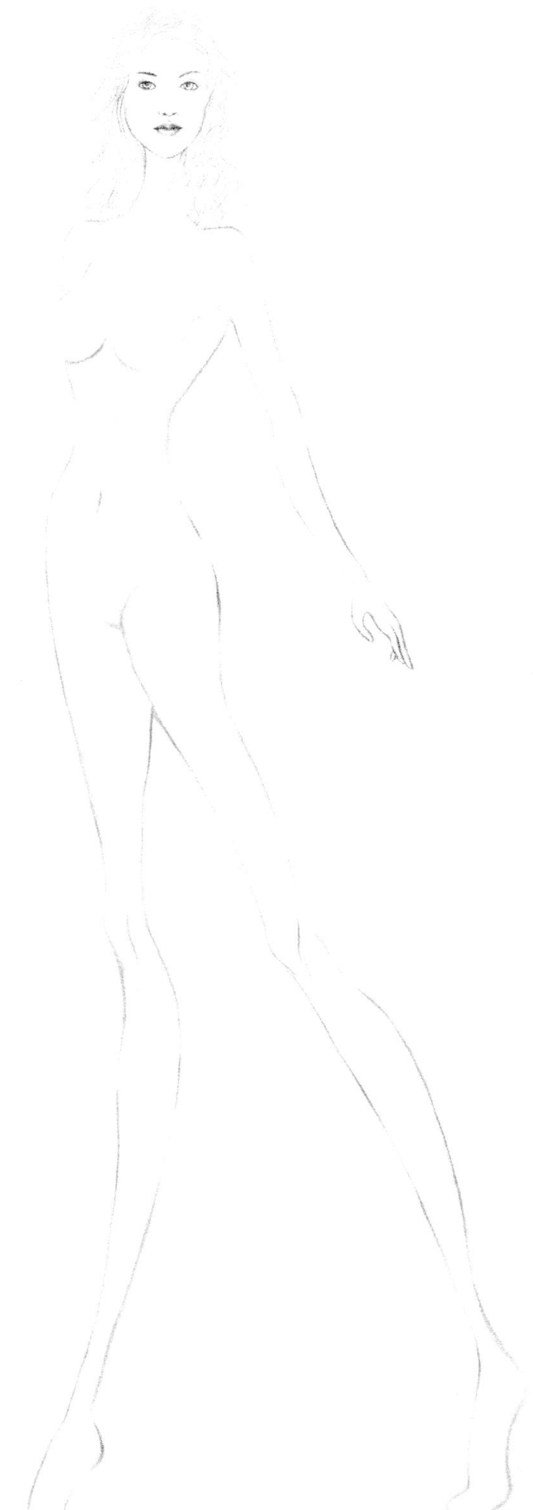

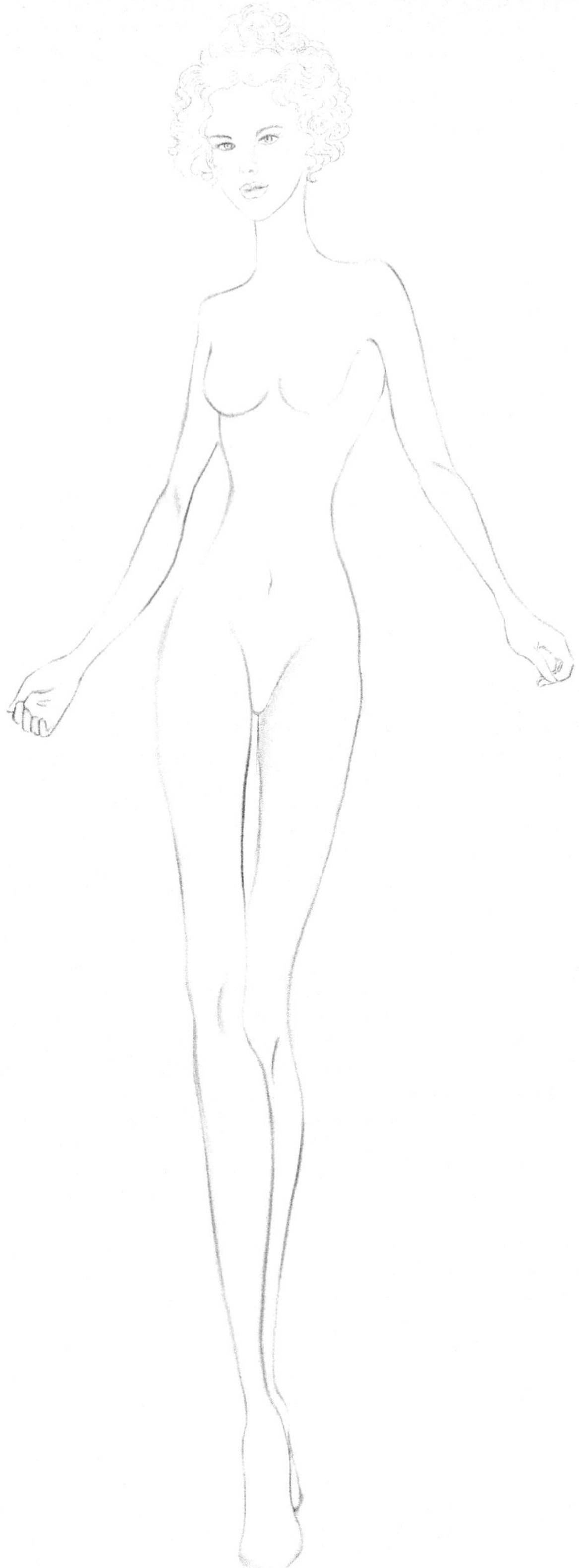

Printed in Great Britain
by Amazon

76025868R00071